Hello Kitty's

little book of big ideas

a girl's guide to brains, beauty, fashion, friendship & fun!

by marie y. moss

HARRY N. ABRAMS, INC., PUBLISHERS

contents

introduction

Want to expand the circumference of your circle of friends? Need advice on hosting a happening? Does your wardrobe need a working-over? No need to sit and stew, because Hello Kitty has gathered a galaxyful of fun-to-follow tips and tricks for getting the most out of all that you do.

Who better to trust for advice than every girl's favorite friend, Hello Kitty? This minuscule mademoiselle packs colossal quantities of experience in everything from finding a forever friend to personalizing your own space. Other advice includes busy-girl beauty tips and fly-girl fashion tricks, ready-to-go travel tactics, and tons of ideas for getting—and keeping—yourself organized.

Now Mama, Papa, your teacher, best friend, or grandma may not be thrilled if you start cutting and coloring your hair and clothes or their favorite magazines, or if you splash paint all over the antique table next to your bed. Always get permission before you start any project—especially one that involves heating devices like the oven or sharp objects such as scissors or knives.

So shout "Hello happiness!" and let Hello Kitty guide you on the art of being a confident and cool twenty-first-century girl.

witty **kitty**

Hello Kitty knows that being smart is cool and that learning new things is fun. When in school, her favorite subjects are English and social studies. In these classes she enjoys reading (especially stories about other girls her age), writing poems, and learning about other cultures. She also enjoys math (and even tutors her sister, Mimmy) and French class *(parlez-vous français?)*.

On her own and outside of school, Hello Kitty learns new things by reading books from the library and by browsing the web for information on topics that interest her (she even keeps a journal listing her favorite books and web sites). She also is a good observer, having already picked up loads of information on topics as varied as planting a garden (from watching and helping the neighbors), training a new pet, and fixing her bicycle.

12 THINGS TO GET YOU THINKING:

1 Keep a pocket dictionary in your backpack and try to learn the definition and spelling of one new word every week.

2 Read the front page and your favorite section of the local newspaper every day (as well as the comics!).

3 Join a library reading club. Find authors that you love, and pledge to read all of their books. If in doubt about where to start: Ask your librarian! He or she will have some super author ideas!

4 Read the biography of someone famous, then try writing your own.

5 Go natural and learn, through research, how to identify the leaves, flowers, and plants found at the park or in your backyard.

6 Plan and research a make-believe family trip. Choose your dream destination or favorite hot spot and determine the best way to travel there and back, where to stay, and what to see. Research this trip well enough, and your family just might take you up on the plan!

7 Be a snoop! Sign on as a reporter for the school newspaper. Don't have a paper at your school? Start your own!

8 Play mind games by stocking up on word games and crossword puzzles.

9 Create a family tree. Begin by gathering stories and pictures from relatives until everything, and everyone, starts to fall into place in history.

10 Write a story with a friend. Start out with a list of fictional characters and their personality traits, then cook up a good tale.

11 Write poems about your friends, family, pets, your feelings and emotions.

12 Join an after-school art class at the library or community center and seek out the true artist within!

Genius tips for cramming, comparing, and concentrating:

1 Keep yourself happy, healthy, and bright-eyed by eating lots of delicious fruit and crunchy vegetables.

smarty **pants**

4 Clear distracting clutter from your school desktop or at-home study area.

3 Snag yourself a quiet area and a comfortable chair for at-home study sessions.

6 Treat yourself to study breaks. Offer to walk Fido and grab some fresh air or head for the kitchen and grab a banana or a glass of cold juice.

8 Make studying more fun with school supplies and creatively covered books. Treat yourself each semester to a fistful of decorated pencils, new notebooks, and a pencil case. Cover schoolbooks in kraft paper (or inside-out grocery-store brown bags) and rubber stamp your own design on them (you can also collage the cover with magazine pictures), or cover each book with a store-bought poster featuring your favorite celebrity.

2 Get lots of mind-clearing sleep.

5 Leave the answering machine on (and turned low) while studying, to avoid distractions.

7 Stand up and say, "I need help" whenever you feel confused or lost about a particular subject, project, or assignment. (*Never* feel embarrassed or ashamed to say, "I just don't get it.")

Hello Kitty's philosophy is that every day presents an opportunity to learn something new and interesting. From signing up to learn to play a new instrument at school to volunteering at the children's zoo, there are many ways to increase, enliven, and broaden your brainpower.

Sometimes these opportunities simply turn up by themselves, like at school, while others need to be discovered on their own. Hello Kitty believes that the best thing about learning is that it makes you smart, and that, in turn, gives you the confidence and courage to be anything you want to be.

style file

It is no secret that Hello Kitty has long been admired

for her unique and playful sense of style. This girl is known for reinventing her

personality every day by dressing each morning to suit her mood. This way,

she can test-drive lots of different characters and develop her own style by the

time she is all grown up. Hello Kitty has Mama to thank for teaching her the

importance of putting together a closet full of wear-'em-all-the-time basics,

but she relies on her own fashion instincts for putting outfits together and

for mixing things up in trendy ways. She also has learned the most important

element of having cool personal style: having confidence in herself.

Some days Hello Kitty feels studious and preppy and shows off this mood by buttoning on a cotton shirt, layering on a cardigan sweater, and pulling on a pair of khaki pants. Accessories and shoes for this mood require a heart locket charm (with a picture of her boyfriend, Daniel, hidden inside) on a silver chain, a tote bag, and a pair of canvas sneakers. Some days Hello Kitty simply feels like being a bit more girlie, so she creates an outfit based on her favorite flower barrette and her long purple skirt.

If it is a high-tech look she is after, she pairs a favorite T-shirt with brightly colored warm-up pants, running shoes, and her metallic backpack. Hello Kitty knows that with a little creativity and experimentation, she can project and try out any number of different personalities.

basics don't have to be BORING

Oh, sure, when Mama first started trying to convince her that a closet full of basics was the best way to begin a well-rounded wardrobe, all Hello Kitty could think was BORING! What could a trendy girl possibly want with a package full of solid T-shirts, ho-hum basic jeans, and a no-style hooded sweatshirt? The answer, she soon saw, was everything. She figured out that these basics were just like the blank canvas of a painter. Hello Kitty could start in search of an outfit by pulling on her own blank canvas of solid essentials, then add colors and textures to individualize her look. The allowance money saved by buying long-lasting basics meant more than a few dollars left over for snapping up trendy accessories, cool notebooks, and a few style-making pieces of clothing to mix things up a bit.

Hello Kitty found that owning good basics makes getting dressed in the morning an easier chore. She's discovered that a closet full of trendy stuff is full of restrictions because trendier pieces often only look good when paired with their matching counterparts. Hello Kitty knows that as fast as trendy clothing comes into style, it goes out of style, so she has decided to rely on clothing that looks good every time out.

FASHION FUNDAMENTALS CHECKLIST:

1 **solid cotton T-shirts**
in a variety of colors (long and short-sleeved)

2 **striped T-shirts**

3 **basic blue jeans**

4 **hooded sweatshirts**
in several colors

5 **a denim jacket**

6 **a drawer full of undies & socks**
of course!

7 **a cotton or wool cardigan sweater**
pick a basic favorite color so you'll want to wear it all the time!

8 **a skirt**
ditto favorite color!

9 **sneakers**
a goes-with-everything canvas pair or trendy running shoes

10 **pretty shoes for dressing up**

11 **pajamas**

12 **slippers**

13 **a warm coat**

14 **a book bag**

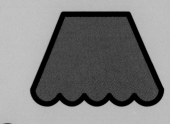

4

8

12

Once Hello Kitty is stocked up on basics, she begins gathering ideas for putting together interesting outfits. She does this by noting the styles of her favorite television and movie actors, by tearing out ideas from fashion magazines and catalogs, and by browsing fashion web sites. Another way she experiments with different mix-and-match schemes is by simply spending an afternoon trying on her things in all possible combinations. She likes to do this once or twice per school semester, and finds that it can be much more fun with a friend who can offer a second opinion. Hello Kitty likes to pull out her instant camera and photograph the looks that make the cut so that she can tape them inside her closet door for easy reference.

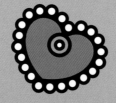

1 Organize

Get your closet in shape to get things started.

4 Dress-down, dress-up pieces

Don't ever be afraid of pairing a favorite T-shirt or denim jacket with a skirt, or wearing sparkly, party-time hair accessories with jeans.

get dressed, girlfriend!

2 Go color crazy

You wouldn't think color combinations like turquoise and purple or pink and brown sound very appealing, but they can be some of the coolest combos out there. Don't be afraid to pull on that baby blue sweater with brown corduroy pants or that red T-shirt with a turquoise necklace.

3 Wear your hair differently

Add a barrette, braid it, go curly to reinvent instantly a tried-and-true outfit.

6 Layer on layer

Put one piece on top of or underneath another to create easy, one-of-a-kind style. Try tying a colorful sweater around your waist when you are wearing a simple T-shirt and jeans or try layering a short-sleeved T-shirt over a fitted long-sleeved T-shirt.

5 Perk things up

Use special little everyday items to add pizzazz. Stock up on a trendy notebook or two for daily classes, a really cool book bag, or a chunky notice-me ring, and they will become your signature pieces.

cheap chic

1 **Visit craft stores** as often as you visit mall accessory stores. Find inspiration at the mall, then buy a bagful of colorful rawhide strings, ribbons, and lots of beads and charms to design your own inexpensive yet trendy accessories.

2 **Throw a swap-meet sleep-over party** and exchange the clothes you've grown tired of with castoffs from your friends' closets. Turn the night into a big fashion show. Donate the rejects to a local charity. (Be sure to get parents' approval beforehand on the items you'd like to swap!)

3 **Visit thrift shops**, secondhand and vintage clothing stores, and tag sales for great buys. Score denim jackets, jeans, wool coats, sweaters, and other interesting one-of-a-kind pieces, some with retro inspirations. (At any given time

there is guaranteed to be something in stores that is the reinvention of a fashion idea from decades ago. For example, in recent years designers have brought back 1950s-inspired Capri pants and cuffed jeans, 1970s corduroy hip hugger pants, and 1980s torn sweatshirts and ripped denim. Take note of what is trendy at the mall and use the phone book or search city web sites to find thrift shops in your neighborhood that may be stocking the originals!)

4 Get parents' approval, then get busy reinventing last year's clothing with a snip or two of the scissors. Give jeans a frayed edge by cutting off a bit of the hem and tossing them into the wash, or find new life in an old shirt by cutting off the sleeves.

Turn old pants into shorts by simply putting them on to measure the length you would like and marking it with a pencil. Take the pants off, fold one leg over the other, and begin snipping across both legs just below the line you have drawn. (Remember, you can always cut them again, but you can't start over once the snipping has begun! It is best to cut a bit longer at first, going back to snip more later if necessary.)

5 Be confident. Creating personal style should never be an expensive project. A simple white T-shirt and blue jeans can be a special fashion statement in itself. Style really comes from having confidence in yourself— and confidence is free!

pretty kitty

Hello Kitty knows that when you feel confident and happy on the inside, you will glow on the outside, too. That is why she tries to eat healthy foods (enjoying a few treats now and then) and gets lots of beauty sleep. She also knows that participating in activities like bike riding and tennis will help keep her healthy and energetic.

Though never one to fuss over her appearance, Hello Kitty enjoys experimenting with different beauty products, and loves to style and create new hairdos for herself and her friends. She likes to keep her look fresh and natural, and she's learned that simple beauty style does not have to be boring. In fact, Hello Kitty knows that the art of primping and pampering is not only fun but can even lift a girl's spirits when she is feeling blue. Whether she is learning to create wavy locks of her own, or doing makeovers on her girlfriends, Hello Kitty knows that practicing and sharing beauty tricks and tips can be a special way to celebrate every girl's individuality.

What every glamour girl needs:

1 scented bubble bath

2 shampoo and conditioner

clean + pretty

silky + shiny

5 moisturizing bath soap

soap

8 cotton swabs

7 clear and tinted nail polish

nail polish

11 nail polish remover

polish off!

12 favorite fragrance

no. 9

3

creamy body moisturizer

4

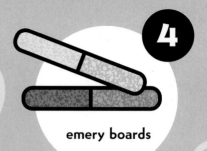

emery boards

beauty basics

6

pretty comb and brush

10

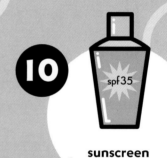

sunscreen

9

lip gloss

13

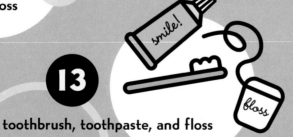

toothbrush, toothpaste, and floss

14

gentle face cleanser

Salon Sleep-over Secrets

Of course miniature golf, pool, and pizza parties are always fun, but Hello Kitty sometimes loves to get things girlie by hosting beauty makeover parties for her girlfriends. Here are a few of her favorite beauty party ideas and activities:

1 Use plain construction paper and a rubber stamp design of a nail polish or perfume bottle to design and decorate your very own invitations.

2 Slip a small lip gloss inside each invitation as a treat.

3 Treat your guests to inexpensive party favors, including fake tattoos or nail decorations, nail polish and emery boards, flavored lip balm, barrettes, and travel-sized shampoos and conditioners.

4 Snap "before" instant photo pictures of guests as they arrive, so they can later compare them to "after" photos.

5 Set up a corkboard to display each girl's set of before and after photos, or send each girl home in the morning with her very own display card of both pictures (simply fold construction paper like a greeting card and tape pictures inside, letting your guests decorate it if desired).

6 Arrange a box or basket full of celebrity pictures and magazine pages that will serve as inspiration for the makeovers.

7 Have each guest select a partner who will help her create the perfect makeover.

8 Arrange for each guest to bring along her makeup bag and hair-styling accessories, or provide each guest with a party favor made up of a small sampling of beauty supplies from the drugstore.

9 Set up a manicure and pedicure area with a comfortable chair, flip-flops, polish remover and cotton balls, and a selection of nail polish colors.

10 Set your computer screen to one of your favorite beauty web sites to encourage beauty browsing, and take advantage of the free, instant advice offered on most sites.

11 Offer a fresh stack of washcloths and towels for cleanup before bedtime.

A bubble bath can be a luxurious way to lounge, but Hello Kitty knows that most busy girls barely have time for a quick shower. Check out these tips for getting the most fun from your next splash 'n dash.

1 *Store your favorite* bath products in a colorful plastic bucket or pail. (With everything stashed in one place, you can just grab the handle and run for the shower the next time you oversleep!)

3 *Remember to keep* temperatures moderate. Every girl loves a hot shower, but Hello Kitty knows that super-scorching water temperatures will dry out her skin.

shower power

2 *Fill a few* small plastic travel bottles with different shampoos and conditioners and keep them all tucked away inside your pail (use a small mailing address sticker to label each bottle). This way you can try a different combination or shampoo scent every day without having to lug around the larger bottles, and you won't have to keep just one bottle at a time in the shower. Do the same for any body scrubs or shower gels.

5 *Add posh* to a quick power shower by using pretty, sweet-smelling soaps.

4 *Conserve your favorite* shampoo by remembering that just a little bit is all you need for a good, thorough shampooing.

1. **Layer** two sheer shades of lip gloss to invent your very own personal shade.

2. **Collect** and carry a little cosmetic case filled with travel-sized items like hand lotion, an emery board, hand sanitizing gel, sunscreen, lip balm, a comb, and clear nail polish so you will be prepared for anything.

3. **Carry** a hair elastic or clip for emergencies so you won't be tempted to use a hair-damaging rubber band.

4. **Keep** nails painted prettily and you'll be less tempted to chew on them at tense moments.

5. **Trust** aromatherapy (the belief that certain scents can induce particular moods) and hit the sack with a lavender sachet tucked underneath your pillow (the lavender scent will calm you into sweet dreams). A glass of warm milk before bedtime might also do the trick.

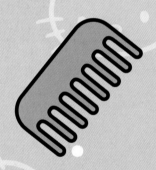

try this!

8 *Treat* rough elbows to a dab of body lotion at bedtime for an overnight softening treatment.

9 *Tuck* a fabric flower inside a ponytail elastic and turn an everyday hairstyle into something sweet and special.

6 *Decorate* basic metal barrettes by painting them with sparkly nail polish. If you are feeling super-creative, cut very small pictures and letters out of magazines and set them in place on a barrette (you can spell out your name, your favorite band, etc.). Now adhere letters and pictures with a thin coat of clear nail polish.

10 *Sign up* for a new haircut at least one week before you have your class picture taken at school. This way you will have time to master the art of styling your new 'do and won't end up unrecognizable in the yearbook.

7 *Try* Hello Kitty's easy trick for creating wavy hair. Tightly twist a small section of wet hair and wind it into a spiral at the scalp, pinning it in place. Repeat with small sections until all hair is pinned up. Leave spirals in overnight, pull pins out in the morning, and wake up to waves!

castle chic

Like most girls, Hello Kitty spends oodles of time in her room, which she considers her castle. Though her room is not very large, she has managed to create a very sweet suite for herself. Hello Kitty's personal space has become just perfect for lounging around, e-mailing friends, studying for tests, or writing in her diary. She likes to keep things neat, though sometimes her days get so busy that a few of her belongings get left out of place. Mama helps out from time to time, but Hello Kitty prides herself on keeping her castle clean and organized.

This girl has got lots of room-decorating tips. She loves color and finds inspiration in rainbows and her well-used box of watercolor paints. When deciding on colors for her room, Hello Kitty tries to create unusual combinations, like pairing green and purple or pink and orange (more often than not, she can be found happily redecorating every three months or so).

Hello Kitty also loves finding new ways to decorate every inch of her bedroom and has become expert at keeping her things organized. She has discovered that when everything is in order, she has more fun enjoying her very own personal space. When it comes to creating a girlfriend-friendly, cheerful room, Hello Kitty's buddies know she can be very resourceful and amazingly creative. From easy-to-make decorations to using store-bought finds, Hello Kitty's got lots of ideas up her sleeve.

paint party!

Hello Kitty's favorite colors are bright springtime shades like pink, yellow, purple, and sky blue. She loves to go to the hardware store with Papa so she can snap up the free-for-the-asking paint color charts and samples that help her decide which colors to choose for her next painting project. Back home, she tapes up the color charts wherever she might eventually like to change the color (like walls, windowsills, and doors). This way she can admire the new colors each day and figure out, over time, which combinations will be her next favorites.

Once she asked Papa to help her paint the windowsills and door a neon pink, keeping the walls white. That looked very special and cheerful. When her friends saw her and Papa's handiwork, they hurriedly hauled home paint to try out this fun color combination. She is already thinking about the next cool color creation for her castle, which might involve painting her ceiling a sunny sky blue—or at least convincing Papa to do it.

color cool

 Turn any wall into a chalkboard with chalkboard paint.

 Paint every wall and ceiling a different color.

 Paint wood floors and doors happy colors, too.

 Add color to your wardrobe by painting the insides of closets and shelves.

 Ditch the headboard on your bed and paint a fake one on the wall.

Any leftover paint gets put away for other fun painting activities like Hello Kitty's terra-cotta pot projects. She loves stocking up on these inexpensive gardening-store finds. With a quick paint job, these perfectly simple pots can become the prettiest storage bins. They always look so sweet on her desk filled with pencils and paper clips as well as on her vanity for storing lip gloss. For Grandparents' Day, she even gave a prettily painted set to Grandma and Grandpa White, who use them for their intended purpose in the backyard country garden. (Grandma White is convinced her pansies grow more quickly in Hello Kitty's painted pots.)

    Other leftover paint projects include painting the wooden frame of a store-bought bulletin or chalkboard, repainting an inexpensive flea market or garage sale table or chair, and reinventing the exterior of a dollhouse with a dip or two of a paintbrush.

Wall Flower

Whenever Hello Kitty changes her paint colors, she can barely wait for the paint to dry so she can redecorate the walls. Over the past few years, decorating her room has become such a fun hobby for her that she's spent lots of time creating new ways to hang decorations.

Hello Kitty loves the feeling of being surrounded by friends, so hanging their pictures is one of her favorite room-decorating do's. Over time she has discovered many ways to frame their fabulous faces. Armed with an instant camera, Hello Kitty loves catching friends off guard. She often tosses her camera into her backpack and hauls it to tennis practice for action shots, to the ice cream parlor for cone-licking candid shots, and into her tomato garden for pretty pictures of her butterfly and ladybug friends. Back at home, she decorates the picture borders by spelling out friends' nicknames in ready-for-gluing letter beads found at the mall. She then gently tapes the photos (overlapping and alternately tilting them right, then left) around the molding of her bedroom windows. She leaves the sills free and clear for knickknacks and storage space. Sometimes Hello Kitty will have her friends sign their pictures, turning her bedroom window into a giant autograph book.

Hello Kitty's mini instant camera and photo booth pictures decorate everything from clear plastic cups (single or multiple stickers turn them into barrette and pushpin storage bins) to plain, unlined notepad paper and envelopes that instantly become personalized stationery.

Hello Kitty loves reading and collecting magazines, so it is only natural that she would find ways to use them in decorating her digs. She loves to frame favorite magazine covers and advertisements, hanging them all along the walls. Those magazines kept intact get stacked up mattress-high and topped with a kitchen tray or other flat item to create one-of-a-kind bedside tables (two stacks side-by-side make a table large enough for a small lamp and some good-night sweets.)

What a girl needs:

✳ **scissors**
even better if you have an extra pair called "pinking shears" that can cut a zigzag edge

✳ **large and small paintbrushes**
rinse them out and they can be used over and over again

✳ **colorful markers**
cheaper by the pack

✳ **ribbon and twine**

✳ **beads**

✳ **tacks**

✳ **glue stick**

✳ **hole puncher**

✳ **tape**

✳ **imagination!**

Make a ribbon bulletin board

What you'll need:

one bulletin board

ribbon in different colors

tacks

scissors

1 Lay the bulletin board down on a flat surface.

2 Tack the end of a piece of ribbon to any corner of the bulletin board (not the frame) and pull the ribbon tautly, on a diagonal, across the board and tack it on the opposite corner.

3 Cut off the excess ribbon.

4 Repeat tacking and cutting ribbons diagonally in this direction, a few inches apart from one another, across entire corkboard surface.

5 Begin tacking ribbons diagonally in the opposite direction, so that ribbons overlap.

6 Tack all spots where ribbons intersect.

7 Insert photos and keepsakes underneath the ribbons.

Hello Kitty Keepers

mall
@
noon!

When her collectibles (like seashells, charm bracelets, dolls, and stickers) threatened to take over her space, Hello Kitty dreamed up ways of storing them without actually putting them away in storage. Her prized seashell collection got gently spilled into one of Mama's large bowls and is kept out for playing, while a few stray shells sit atop her bookshelf for instant admiring and for daydream sessions of her summers at the beach. Her charm bracelet collection gets happily stowed inside one of Grandma White's old floral-covered sewing boxes. (If there is anything Hello Kitty has learned about room storage, it is that decorated boxes and bins can actually make storing a decorating art in itself.) Finding storage space for Hello Kitty's dolls and toys was a breeze once she stumbled upon Grandpa White's stash of cardboard boxes in his garage. He let her take two flat boxes home with her, and she decorated them with pictures cut out from her favorite magazines. She overlapped the pictures to create a large collage. Both boxes got filled with Hello Kitty's collectibles and have found an out-of-the-way home underneath her bed.

Hello Kitty's stickers get stashed inside plastic sandwich bags, categorized by color and theme. All the bags are stored inside one of Hello Kitty's monogrammed canvas totes, which is kept next to her desk for quick sticker access.

Schoolwork, friends' phone numbers, postcards, and greeting cards are displayed in the most unusual ways in Hello Kitty's room. One of her favorite ideas for organizing these little reminders and notes is to hang a mini clothesline right inside her room! She tacks a strand of twine or skinny rope across the back of her bedroom door and uses her dolls' small colorful clothespins or tiny clips from the stationery store to clip up little notes or keepsakes.

Small Ideas, Big Impact

1 Line dresser drawers and closet shelves with brightly colored tissue paper.

2 Tie-dye plain white sheets and pillowcases (score inexpensive dyeing kits at the supermarket, and follow the easy instructions).

3 Use a wicker basket as a deskside wastepaper basket.

4 Paint or decorate clothespins and use them as large paper clips.

5 Store stuff away in old doll clothes cases.

6 Stash compact discs in a decorated shoe box.

7 Jot down notes and reminders on an old chalkboard.

8 Stow your favorite shower gel and shampoo in a colorful plastic beach pail.

9 Turn an old bicycle basket into a standing desk file for school notes and folders.

10 Liven up wire hangers by wrapping them in ribbon, fabric, or pipe cleaners.

Totally Tropical

Hello Kitty's all-time favorite decoration idea helped her turn her wintertime bedroom into a sunny tropical paradise. Having discovered inexpensive straw hula skirts at the local party shop, she quickly snipped one into fringe (five or six inches long) and tacked it right up onto the front of the windowsills. Then she planted small amounts of Grandma White's grass seed in some of her painted pots and lined them on the windowsill to give the room a summery feel (she just snipped the grass every week or so as it grew). Her wildest idea was to add a plastic grasslike doormat at the foot of her bed! And to complete the tropical spirit, Hello Kitty often tagged along with Mama on trips to the fabric and craft store, where she picked wire-stemmed flowers to twist around her desk chair, headboard, curtain rod, and doorknobs.

Beach Baby

think sand and sea colors, a bowl full of goldfish, seashells, sheer curtains, vacation postcards, flip-flops worn as slippers year round

Snow Princess

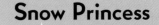

think pale blue and white colors, ice skates hung over the bedpost, mittens-on-a-string around the doorknob, a bowl of white peppermint candies, skis propped in the corner, a big fluffy feather-filled comforter

theme scheme inspirations

Friendly Futuristic

think metallic colors mixed with white, silver picture frames, copper-colored markers, geometric printed bedding, tag sale chairs spray-painted silver

Outside Inside

think butterfly color combinations like purple and yellow or green and blue, a comfy camp sleeping bag used in place of a comforter, windowsill pansies, a bowl of acorns, leaves pinned to a bulletin board

Color Crazy

think bright color mixes like turquoise and fuchsia, multicolored satin floor pillows, strings of patio lights with colorful bulbs, framed magazine covers, color-coordinated clothing in the closet, brightly painted flea market furniture

10 Tag Sale & Thrift Shop Treasures

1

Vintage luggage
makes excellent pack-it-away storage for notebooks and stationery

2

Old pins and brooches
are perfect for using as bulletin board pushpins

5

Glass jars with lids
store just about anything

8

Bandannas and cotton scarves
liven up an old pillow by placing one scarf over the front of the pillow and another scarf over the back and tying the ends into knots

9

Weathered chairs, tables, and bookshelves
get new life with a fresh coat of paint

3

Plastic charms

tie onto presents, or make jewelry
by attaching them to a colorful
string or ribbon

4

Beaded necklaces

are pretty—or pull them
apart and glue the beads onto
a picture frame

6

Magazines and old greeting cards

can be cut up to make collages or
to decorate gift boxes, envelopes,
and boxes, or frame your favorite
pages and cutouts

7

Old sewing and craft supplies

use sewing boxes and bins for storage,
and stock up on multipurpose ribbons,
pipe cleaners, and buttons for future
decorating projects

10

Seashells

flip them over and store small jewelry
or paper clips inside, or use larger shells
as summertime paperweights

pal power

Hello Kitty considers every true friend a member of her family. Each one is special for some unique quality. She cannot imagine her happy life without so many caring pals and knows that good friends come in all shapes, colors, and sizes. A potential best buddy might be found in that shy, sweet girl from art class or in that new boy who just moved into the house down the street. Hello Kitty has discovered that sometimes all it takes is a simple "hello" to start a conversation that might lead to a lasting friendship.

Hello Kitty treasures some friends for their playful, carefree spirits. These pals are always fun to be around, keeping her in stitches with funny tales, jokes, and riddles. At the first sign of worry, Hello Kitty knows she can turn to these friends for upbeat phone chats and activities that will free her head of anything that might be getting her down. Other friends can be relied upon for their adventurous spirits. These pals urge Hello Kitty to try new things (like snowboarding, auditioning for school plays, or learning gymnastics). Other friends are simply calm and quiet and have a soothing effect on Hello Kitty when she is feeling anxious or nervous about taking history tests or competing in tennis matches. Overall, Hello Kitty believes that true forever friends should be cherished for their honesty, kindness, and respect for others. Her absolute best friends understand the importance of keeping shared secrets, of being loyal, and of only wanting the best of everything for one another. And Hello Kitty realizes that to make and keep good friends, she must be a good friend, too!

Hello Kitty's tips for being the best friend that you can be:

buddy basics

♥ Be a good listener.

♥ Be honest.

♥ Treat friends just as you would like to be treated yourself.

♥ Let friends know you are thinking of them with phone calls, e-mails, and letters.

♥ Use your confidence in particular areas to help others. Coach a friend to shoot a basketball free throw, tutor a pal on your favorite school subject, or help a buddy who has very little cash find the perfect bargain party dress and accessories.

♥ Remember special days like birthdays by keeping notes in a friendship journal.

♥ Include a shy classmate in your conversations and activities.

♥ Arrange get-togethers to introduce one group of friends to another.

♥ Never gossip.

♥ Plan events and outings that include both your friends and your family so that each will learn to feel comfortable with the other.

Daniel
kind and sensitive

Tracy
mischievous

Tippy
sweet and strong

Kathy
considerate

Kitty's caboodle of friends

Thomas
busy as a bee and always
on the move

Jody
studious and determined

Fifi
precocious

Mimmy
daydreamer

Lorry
mysterious

Joey
athletic and patient

LITTLE PAL PLEASERS

hello friend

1. **Pack** an extra dessert in your school lunch bag.

2. **Tape** a traveling friend's favorite television show.

3. **Write** a personalized friendship poem.

4. **Tie** balloons to a friend's front porch to celebrate a birthday or a special accomplishment like getting an A on a book report or making the swim team.

5. **Treat** for popcorn at the movies.

6. **Loan** your bicycle to a friend without one.

7. **Invite** a new classmate to join you and your friends on an after-school snack hunt or shopping spree.

8. **Mail** a small souvenir from your vacation to a lonely friend back home.

9. **Ask** someone to take a group photo of you and your friends. Make color copies of the picture and frame them and give them to everyone as a special holiday gift.

10. **Help** a friend with a not-so-fun chore. Garage cleanup and lawn care might call for a few good compact discs and a portable stereo. Accompany a friend on an after-school dog walk and use the time to catch up on the day's events.

friend trips

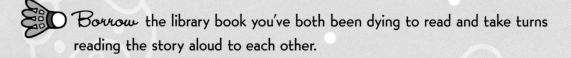

Pal-perfect plans for spending time together:

🐾 *Borrow* the library book you've both been dying to read and take turns reading the story aloud to each other.

🐾 *Volunteer* together at the community center. Teach arts and crafts, or read to a kindergarten group.

🐾 *Baby-sit* as a team.

🐾 *Visit* a new exhibit at an art museum.

🐾 *Learn* a sport together.

🐾 *Browse* a flea market and surprise each other with a cheap treat or two.

🐾 *Share* french fries and a milkshake at the counter of the local diner.

🐾 *Plan* a biking picnic trip. Eat at stops along the way, and save dessert for your final destination.

🐾 *Surprise* your pal by turning Friday night into a film festival. Get set by renting a few of your friend's favorite flicks and stocking up on microwave popcorn and licorice. Keep her guessing at the movie titles till she sees the opening credits.

🐾 *Choose* the same summer camp and greet the great outdoors with your buddy.

what's cookin'

In Hello Kitty's house, the kitchen

is not only the place to prepare and enjoy meals, but it is also the homework

hot spot and the always-active family room. The entire Hello Kitty clan and

their friends enjoy the welcoming comfort of the kitchen more than any other

room in the house.

Mama's weekly batch of made-from-scratch cookies might explain this

kitchen's appeal or the fact that cooking and baking are some of the family's

favorite hobbies. (Hello Kitty often gets lessons from Mama in apple pie and

cupcake baking, and when Grandma White visits, Hello Kitty likes to sit in on

the soup-making sessions.) Whether learning to prepare an old family recipe,

serving up after-soccer treats for friends, or studying alone at the table with

a bag of pretzels and pop, Hello Kitty finds the quiet, familiar comfort of her

kitchen incomparable.

Ingredients for the first-time chef:

Begin your chef-in-training role with a few pieces of your very own kitchen equipment. Stock up on the next family trip to the grocery store or search for one-of-a-kind vintage kitchen treasures at a flea market. Try to have these items in place before signing on as kitchen apprentice:

* apron
* bandanna or barrette to hold hair back
* measuring cups and spoons
* spatula (for scooping out and testing Mama's chocolate icing)
* kitchen timer
* wooden spoons of different lengths
* pot holders
* cookie cutters

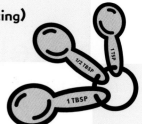

Now follow Hello Kitty's tips and ideas for lending a helping hand:

1   Help gather recipe ingredients before getting started.

2   Offer to squeeze lemons when recipes call for lemon juice or to twist oranges on the fruit juicer for breakfast.

3   Mix ingredients with a wooden spoon in a big mixing bowl.

4   Help smooth icing onto cupcakes or cakes.

5   Roll out dough with a rolling pin.

6   Cut shapes out of dough with cookie cutters.

7   Place spoon-size dollops of cookie mixture onto cookie sheets to prepare for baking.

8   Measure out spices or dry baking ingredients.

9 Wash vegetables.

10 Pour pie fillings into shells or place and pinch top crusts onto pies.

11 Hang around to help with the kitchen cleanup.

Recipe for Fun

Hello Kitty looks forward to the time when she can whip up specialties on her own, but until then she has found many fun ways to help Mama and Grandma in the kitchen. She has also experimented in developing her own creative cooking ideas (always with Mama's supervision) and has happily discovered that some of her kitchen tricks have made their way into the family recipe file. Here are some of her favorite tips—try them!

1 Make fruity ice cubes by pouring juice into ice cube trays and freezing them.

2 Use cookie cutters on bread and cheese slices to create designer sandwiches.

3 Personalize a peanut butter sandwich by adding sliced banana.

4 Treat yourself to breakfast cereal with chocolate milk.

5 Sprinkle Parmesan cheese on a bowl of hot popcorn.

6 Flip over fish sticks by dipping them in a variety of sauces like spicy mustard, or cocktail or barbecue sauce.

7 Decorate birthday cupcakes with edible treats like jelly beans and gummy candy.

8 Top off a bowl of ice cream with your favorite crunchy cereal.

9 Freeze to please when you keep a bunch of grapes in the freezer.

10 Stir hot cocoa with a peppermint stick for minty flavor.

the perfect **picnic**

1 Wash raw vegetables (like celery or carrots) and tuck them in small zippered food storage bags. Fill small plastic containers with creamy salad dressing, yogurt, or sour cream for dipping.

3 Wash fresh fruit and pack with ice to keep cool. Try seedless grapes and apple or orange slices.

4 Fill a thermos full of lemonade. Bring along a few cherries or strawberries to garnish each cupful.

6 Toss together a small bag of hard-to-melt mixed candy treats such as string licorice, fruit chews, and gummy fish.

2 Make a variety of individually wrapped sandwiches. Serve up classics like peanut butter and jelly or American cheese but toss in a few more unusual sandwich recipes for your more adventurous picnic pals. Try pita pocket bread stuffed with sprouts, diced tomato, bits of cheese, and salad dressing, or mozzarella with olive spread on a baguette.

5 Bake or buy brownies or cookies for dessert (or stash away a few dollars and simply flag down the ice cream truck).

DON'T FORGET TO PACK:

 blanket
one that can later be thrown in the wash

 recyclable plastic plates and cups
(wash them and use them again!), napkins, and utensils

 music
portable stereo or radio

 games and sports equipment

 garbage bags for easy cleanup
don't forget a recycling bag

 bug spray!

 picnic basket, plastic containers, and sandwich bags
and if you are not eating right away, be sure you tuck an ice pack in with perishable food such as yogurt, cheese, and salad dressing to keep it cold.

Lemonade

What you'll need for approximately six glasses:

pitcher

measuring cup

fruit juicer

six glasses

6 cups water

½ cup sugar

4 lemons

ice cubes

lemon slices

Pour water into pitcher. Stir in sugar. Squeeze lemons and add juice to water. Stir. Taste and determine if more water or sugar is needed. Serve each glass of lemonade with ice and a lemon slice to decorate.

Kitty's Cookies

What you'll need:

baking sheet

nonstick pan spray

roll of frozen cookie dough (any flavor)

mini cookie cutters

spatula

cooling rack

Ask an adult to preheat the oven (check cookie dough package for temperature) and help you slice the cookie dough. Cut shapes out of slices with a variety of cookie cutter shapes. Spray baking sheet with nonstick spray and place each cookie cutout on the baking sheet a few inches apart from the others (cookies will expand while baking). Keep an adult around to check baking progress and to remove baking sheet when cookies are done. Let cookies cool on cooling rack for about twenty minutes. Munch a few yourself (a reward for all your hard work!), then wrap six at a time in colored tissue paper and tuck them inside party favor takeout containers. Attach a gift tag and a mini cookie cutter to the wire handles and you've got a yummy homemade gift.

travel time

Hello Kitty loves to travel, even if it means simply spending the weekend at Grandma and Grandpa White's home in the country. Though she has traveled longer distances with her family, Hello Kitty has discovered that whether you are visiting near or far, there is always something new and exciting to be learned from the journey.

The most fun in traveling is getting to see how others dress and speak, what they eat, and how they spend their day. Whether it is Grandpa White's neighbors making pizza on the barbecue or roadside vendors selling fresh-picked strawberries from the back of wheelbarrows, Hello Kitty loves to observe and has learned to appreciate and celebrate the differences she discovers in others and their surroundings.

get packin'

A happy trip starts with good planning. When Hello Kitty learns of a trip to her grandparents or a family vacation, the first thing she does is jot down the upcoming travel date in her daybook. This adds to the excitement and anticipation of the trip, because every day she can count down to the departure. Hello Kitty prepares for her excursions in many other ways, too. Check out her list for planning the perfect getaway.

1 **Mark the days** that you will be away from home on your calendar. By doing this you can determine if appointments like music lessons or computer classes will need to be rescheduled.

2 **Start saving** for souvenirs. If you have had trouble saving your allowance, ask around the neighborhood to see if there are any odd jobs that you can do for small fees. Neighbors might need help with lawn care or a car wash, while your own family might find extra chores for you to help out with like laundry or cleaning the basement.

3 **Snoop around** for any special clothing you might need on your trip. Mama might have packed away your ski equipment, or you might need to dig your summer clothes out of the attic. Figure out ahead of time which items might need repairing or cleaning.

4 **Write a list** of the clothing, shoes, and accessories you will need for each day you will be away. Don't forget to pack for special events like fancy dinners, days spent at the pool, or sports.

Design personalized name tags for your luggage. You can decorate cardboard tags found at a stationery store with stickers or rubber stamps or use cardboard, a hole punch, and some string to fashion your very own from scratch. Have tags coated with plastic covers, or laminated, at the local photo shop.

Check out faraway forecasts on weather web sites so that you can pack appropriately.

Find a caring friend or neighbor to provide pets with food and companionship while you are away.

Turn a simple notebook into a travel journal so you will have a special place to record everything you see and do on your trip. Simply decorate the notebook cover with stickers, rubber stamps, or drawings inspired by your upcoming destination, and tuck an envelope inside to store cards and trinkets you might acquire on the road. Think of it as your travel diary.

Check camera batteries and be sure to pack film for your personal camera or arrange in advance to borrow one from a friend.

Determine whether the trip requires a simple overnight backpack or sturdy luggage.

Stock up on postcard stamps if you plan on sending news and views back home to family and friends.

Jot yourself a reminder to pack vitamins, allergy pills, or sunscreen.

Prepare to pack a fun book or two, a deck of cards, crossword puzzles, compact disc player and CDs, and pen-pal stationery for downtime on the trip.

Bring along a favorite pillow or bedtime stuffed animal that might make sleeping away from home a bit more comfortable.

Hello Kitty's favorite cities

Though most of her knowledge of faraway cities comes from browsing travel web sites and from reading and dreaming of exotic destinations, Hello Kitty has already determined her top six picks for the places she would most like to visit. Dream of your own future cross-country road trip, island-hopping cruise, or international excursion using Hello Kitty's picks for inspiration.

New York City. What girl could resist a trip to the best shopping destination in the world? Hello Kitty hears that this city is just brimming with wonderful stores, boutiques, and streetside vendors, all offering the best of everything. Once the shopping is done, there are theater tickets to score, city sites to visit (Statue of Liberty, Empire State Building, and museums, to name a few), and a multicultural mix of neighborhoods that will have any girl feeling oh-so-international without ever having to leave the country. What would Hello Kitty pack? Comfortable walking shoes, a subway map, and a roomy backpack to store her city-girl finds while scouting uptown, downtown, and everywhere in between.

Chicago. Hello Kitty hears this friendly city is worth visiting for its stuffed pizza and hot dogs (called "red hots" by the locals), pretty Lake Michigan views, and a trip to the tippy-tops of the John Hancock

building and the Sears Tower. More Windy City plans would include a trip to one of Illinois's year-round weekend flea markets and a visit to the famous Field Museum. Take-'em-home souvenirs would include a poster from the Art Institute of Chicago and a snow globe from the flea market.

Los Angeles. Home of Hollywood and land of celebrities, Hello Kitty hopes a future West Coast trip will include television and movie studio tours and lots of movie star sightings! She would absolutely have to see the actual Hollywood sign in the hills and would hope for a glimpse of destinations just outside the city, like Malibu Beach and the famous Venice Beach boardwalk. Hello Kitty has read that thrift store shopping in Los Angeles is fab, especially for scoring retro dresses and accessories from the 1940s and 1950s. She has also heard that glamour-girl shopping in Beverly Hills is a super-shopper's dream. What's for lunch on this West Coast excursion? The healthy diet of many West Coast girls would call for a mango and raspberry fruit smoothie and a fresh tossed salad.

Paris. This city is home to many wonderful art museums, including the Louvre, which houses Leonardo da Vinci's famous painting *Mona Lisa*.

Bonjour France!

After a day or two of visiting museums, Hello Kitty would climb the Eiffel Tower, take a boat ride down the Seine (a river that runs right through the city), and snap up some delicious pastries and French perfume. A dinnertime must-do would be to dine at an outdoor café for *pommes frites* (french fries) and people-watching.

Tokyo. Hello Kitty knows this city is a very long airplane ride away, but she just knows it will be worth the trip. Her wish list of sites to see include the Tokyo Tower observation deck and the world-famous Ueno Park Zoo. She would also plan a boat ride down Tokyo Bay and a lightning-fast ride on the city's monorail. No trip to Tokyo would be complete without shopping excursions to the trendy neighborhood of Harajuku and a stop at an authentic Tokyo sushi bar. Souvenirs would include Japan's delicious and colorfully packaged cookies and treats, found in Tokyo's local grocery stores.

London. First stop would definitely be a visit to the queen. That means an underground train ride to Buckingham Palace to see the changing of the guard. Hello Kitty's Brit hits include a visit to Big Ben, London Bridge, and the Tower of London (to see the sparkly royal jewels!), and shopping excursions down King's Road and through Covent Garden. Lunch would require traditional fish and chips and malt vinegar with a famous English chocolate bar for dessert.

RUSSIA

you have arrived

Hello Kitty has learned to take full advantage of the things new places and situations have to offer her. Follow her tips, and you'll be sure to arrive back home with many exciting tales and adventures to share. (You might even begin applying some of her travel tips to your everyday life on home turf.)

1. **Pay attention to detail.** Act like a newspaper reporter and look beyond the big picture to notice the little details. Be aware of things like the aroma of the meadows, the way people your age dress or the music they listen to, how the local menus differ from the restaurants back home, and what families do together in the evenings or on the weekends.

2. **Document discoveries** in your travel journal each night before going to bed.

3. **Try new things.** Make a pact with yourself to make discoveries beyond what you are used to eating, doing, and thinking. Key lime pie and gnocchi might sound strange but are certainly worth one small bite. Use this same advice for test-driving new games and sports and for befriending those whom you might otherwise dismiss.

4. **Scoop up** one particular type of souvenir in every city you visit and you will have begun the collection of a lifetime. Ideas to get you started include metal statues like the Eiffel Tower, Statue of Liberty, or the Sears Tower, postcards (new and vintage), and snow globes.

5. **Develop photos** before you head for home, so you can share your trip with friends and family immediately upon your return.

you go, girl!

There now, are you feeling inspired? Are you ready to see, do, write, read, play, and explore? Begin a to-do list created from your favorite Hello Kitty highlights in this book. Over time, you will want to add your very own tips, tricks, and ideas for easy reference. Take your time mapping out plans, stay organized, recruit friends, and most important, have fun!

Now maintain the momentum by starting a small Hello Kitty project right away, and let that enthusiasm build into bigger adventures. Remember that with gal pal Hello Kitty in tow, every cool, confident twenty-first-century girl will find a pleasing palette of possibilities in each new day.

Design by Higashi Glaser

Although we created this book digitally, it began with the same creative process as traditional artistic media: hand-drawn "thumbnail" sketches on tracing paper. These mini-illustrations of each page let us design situations for Hello Kitty, set the style and flow of the book, and help us visualize our overall concept. To reflect the bold simplicity and light-hearted attitude of Hello Kitty, we selected a bright, soft color palette, and designed cheery iconographic patterns to create a chock-full-of-fun world.

Library of Congress Cataloging-in-Publication Data

Moss, Marie.

Hello Kitty's little book of big ideas : a girl's guide to brains, beauty, fashion, friendship & fun! / by Marie Moss.
    p.   cm.

ISBN 0-8109-4158-9 (Abrams: hardcover)/ISBN 0-8109-9053-9 (book club: pbk)

1. Girls—Life skills guides—Juvenile literature. 2. Grooming for girls—Juvenile literature.
[1. Girls. 2. Life skills. 3. Friendship. 4. Beauty, Personal. 5. Time management.] I. Title.

HQ777.M69 2001
646.7'00835'2—dc21   00-049593

HARRY N. ABRAMS, INC.
100 FIFTH AVENUE
NEW YORK, N.Y. 10011
www.abramsbooks.com